THE PENDLE WITCHES

BY

WALTER BENNETT, M.A.

AUTHOR OF

'The History of Burnley'

First published — 1957 by
The County Borough of Burnley
Libraries & Arts Committee.

Published, 1976-90 by
L.C.C. Library and
Leisure Committee

This edition published by
Lancashire County Books, 1993

Copyright © W. Bennett, 1957.

Printed by T. Snape & Co. Ltd., Preston.

THE PENDLE WITCHES

To all who live within a few miles of Pendle Hill, the mention of the Pendle Witches rouses a special interest. In the popular mind, a witch was a woman who had sold her soul to the Devil and, accompanied often by an evil spirit in the shape of a cat or dog, could cast spells, raise storms, ride through the skies on a broom-stick, provide herself with warmth, food and light, and had the power to kill or maim men and cattle; often she was pictured dancing round a seething cauldron of loathsome brew or maliciously making clay images of the people she wished to kill. In actual fact, a so-called witch was usually a withered old woman, often mentally deranged or disfigured by some physical malformation. In all cases, she was feared for her reputed evil powers and children fled at her approach. The "Witch Scenes" in Shakespeare's Macbeth summed up the popular conception of witchcraft.

In general, "Old Demdike" and "Old Chattox", the two oldest and most notorious of the local witches, have retained their traditional character but the popular view of Anne Redfern, Alice Nutter, Elizabeth Davies and her three children, Alizon, James and Jenet, has been greatly influenced by Harrison Ainsworth's "Lancashire Witches" and Robert Neill's more recent "Mist over Pendle". Both these books are remarkably well written novels and give a clear picture of the contemporary life of the district but, for the sake of drama and romance, the writers have introduced situations and characters which do not form a part of the original story.

The Pendle Witches lived during the reigns of Elizabeth I 1558-1603 and James I 1603-1625. The only source of information about what really occurred is a book called "The Wonderful Discoverie of Witches in the Countie of Lancaster", written and published by Mr. Thos. Potts in November 1612, three months after the execution of the witches. Potts was the Clerk to the Judges of the Lancaster Assize of 1612 and it was on their instructions that the book was issued. It contains the depositions and confessions of the accused which were made at the Magistrate's Court as well as the evidence of witnesses at the

3

Assize Court; above all, it expresses the editor's personal views that the "witches" were murderers and that their foul crimes merited the death sentence which was so rightly imposed by his masters on the judicial bench. He eulogises the Judges and concludes "that God Almightie hath singled them out and set them on his Seat, for the defence of Justice; and for this great deliverance, let us pray to God Almightie, that the memorie of these worthie Judges may be blessed to all Posterities". From the writer of such fulsome praise, one can hardly expect an unbiassed and critical account of the history of the Pendle Witches.

Before examining the evidence against the witches as transcribed by Potts from the official documents, it is necessary to learn something of the local conditions that existed at the time. Superstition was widespread among all classes of society. Wells, ponds and even groups of stones were thought to be the haunts of fairies, elves and goblins, while evil spirits roamed the countryside seeking opportunities to inflict injuries of every sort from maiming cattle and killing men to spoiling ale and butter and preventing bread from rising. Often amulets and charms, such as a horse shoe, a holed stone or a circle of rowan twigs fastened to the door of a cottage or shippon, could be effective against the designs of the evil one. A small piece of parchment on which were written the names of the Trinity, Greek and Roman gods, planets, mystical signs and a Latin prayer, was often worn round the neck to guard a person from disaster; even a monk of Whalley thought it well worth while to write down a charm against toothache and another one to stop bleeding. It was also believed that evil spirits sometimes took possession of the bodies of children, made them undergo bodily contortions and lose consciousness, and could only be expelled by the prayers of a godly minister. Several such cases of demoniacal possession are recorded locally but that of 1596 in which two grandchildren of Edmund Starkie of Huntroyd were the victims is important because Roger Nowell of Read Hall, who had so much to do with the Pendle Witches, was a near neighbour of the Starkies. The children exhibited all the signs of epilepsy but Nowell would certainly believe that their condition was due to evil spirits.

People who could believe in the corporeal existence of evil spirits accepted without question the wildest tales about the powers and activities of those persons who were reputed to have personal connections with the Devil's agents so that a sudden

4

death, a prolonged illness, or a loss on a farm was attributed to the evil designs of some witch or other. King James I believed so thoroughly in witchcraft and the need to eradicate it that he wrote and published in 1597 a book called "Daemonologie" which ranked as a textbook on the subject. Under its influence, an Act was passed in 1604 which imposed the death penalty for making a covenant with an evil spirit, using a corpse for magic, hurting life or limb, procuring love or injuring cattle by means of charms. The Judges at the trial at Lancaster, James Altham and Edward Bromley, seem to have been biassed against the prisoners for they did not point out the serious contradictions given in the evidences of witnesses and encouraged the star witness for the prosecution, Jenet Davies, a child of nine, to give evidence against her own mother, brother and sister, and neglected to challenge the veracity of the young girl except by an artifice that any child of normal intelligence would have immediately recognised as a trap. By publishing an account of the trial which resulted in the deaths of eight unfortunate people, they hoped to impress the King with their zeal and determination to stamp out all forms of witchcraft. The prosecutor at Lancaster Assize was Roger Nowell of Read Hall who, as a local magistrate, had already made a preliminary examination, written out with his own hand the depositions and confessions, and had finally sent twelve witches to Lancaster and one to York to await trial at the next Assizes. Little is known about him except that he was a wealthy landowner, had been High Sheriff of Lancaster in 1610 and was fond of litigation; he was most probably responsible for building up the whole affair of the Pendle Witches out of a few wild accusations made against Old Demdike by a young girl who was herself a convicted thief.

Another feature is the abject poverty of all but one of the witches. Poverty in Pendle Forest had been common for many years and in the early part of the 16th century two women of Barley had been excused attendance at Church because they had no clothes to wear. Conditions were no better in the early 17th century, e.g. Demdike on one occasion sat in her house wearing only a single garment; Demdike, Alizon and James Davies, Chattox and Anne Redfern were always begging or stealing; only two of the witches are recorded as having done any work at all. Most of the witches were undesirable characters for in addition to their laziness and ignorance, at least three of them were mothers of illegitimate children.

5

Two families, Demdike and Chattox, provided the most important of the reputed witches.

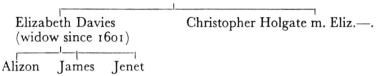

Elizabeth Southern nicknamed "Demdike"

Elizabeth Davies	Christopher Holgate m. Eliz.—.
(widow since 1601)	

Alizon James Jenet

Elizabeth Southern or "Demdike" was in 1612 an old woman of eighty and completely blind. She confessed to having been a witch for twenty years and said that she first met a spirit or devil in the shape of a boy near a stonepit at Newchurch as she was coming home from begging, and that six years later the spirit, named "Tibb", came to her as a dog and sucked her blood, after which she was "stark mad" for eight weeks.

Elizabeth Davies suffered from a facial malformation in that her eyes were unevenly set—one looked up and the other downwards. She was probably mentally unstable and subject to fits of uncontrollable passion. She said her spirit was named "Ball".

Christopher Holgate, an illegitimate son of Demdike, lived with his wife near Pendle Hill. Nothing of importance is known about them except that they were said to be witches though they were not tried for witchcraft at the great trial in 1612.

Alizon Davies was perhaps the most intelligent of her family but it was her misfortune that brought so much trouble to them; she seems to have made a living by begging.

James Davies, a youth of weak and childish intellect, inclined to be vicious but frightened by authority, was ready to give any evidence that would suit the magistrates; he was apparently incapable of working, always begging and a thief. He stated that his spirit was named "Dandy" which in the shape of a brown dog first met him near Newchurch.

Jenet Davies was about nine years of age in 1612, pert, precocious and anxious to draw attention to herself. Desirous of creating an impression, she was ready to swear away the lives of every member of her family. In 1633, she herself was imprisoned as a witch.

Demdike lived with her daughter and grandchildren in a house or converted building called "Malkin Tower" which was situated in Malkin Field, part of Sadler's Farm, Newchurch. Some five hundred yards away from Malkin Tower and less than thirty minutes' walk for a blind old woman was Bull Hole Farm where Demdike made an unsuccessful attempt to cure a

6

sick cow and where Chattox is said to have tried to charm milk
she had begged from the farm. Also at a very short distance
from Malkin Tower was Moss End, the home of John and Jane
Bulcock, two of the witches tried at Lancaster.

The Chattox family was as follows:

Anne Whittle nicknamed "Chattox"

Anne Redfern, a widow in 1612   Elizabeth (Bessie)

Mary

Thomas Potts describes the head of the family thus: "This
Anne Whittle, alias Chattox, was a very old withered spent and
decreped creature, her sight almost gone . . . Her lippes ever
chattering and walking; but no man knew what". Her spirit or
familiar was called "Fancy". It is uncertain whether the
nickname of "Chattox" is a corruption of "Chatterbox"
referring to her habit of mumbling or talking to herself, or a
variation of the surname of "Chadwick"; a Clitheroe document
of 1626 which contains the words "Anne, thou art a Chadwick
and a Demdike" suggests the latter origin.

Anne Redfern, daughter of Chattox, was described as "more
dangerous than her mother for she made all or most of the
Pictures of Clay, that were made or found at any time".

Elizabeth or Bessie Chattox, another daughter, was a convicted
thief and seems to have been the person whose spiteful accusations made to Roger Nowell led to the magistrate's preliminary enquiries, the trial at Lancaster and the final scenes on the scaffold.

The Chattox family lived in a cottage near a stream in West
Close, i.e. the district between Higham and the River Calder. It
was in this district that several of the 1633 witches lived, possibly
near Pendle Hall and Hunterholme. The house of the Chattox family was situated on land belonging to the Nutters of Greenhead.

The first official enquiry into the activities of the Pendle
Witches took place at Read Hall on March 13th 1612. One
wonders why action had not been taken before that date if all
or any of the stories about their practices were true. Demdike,
according to Mr. Potts, had been a witch for fifty years,
Elizabeth Davies stated that her mother had had "a mark" for
forty years, though Demdike herself would admit to only
twenty years during which she had practised her evil arts.
Taking 1610 as the date of her last reputed "killing", why was
nothing done by the parish officials before 1612 and why was
no relative of the deceased then called to give evidence? Again,

7

it was only in 1612 that Chattox was accused of murdering two men, one in 1593 and the other in 1595, and again one wonders why their relatives had kept silence for so many years. Obviously, something must have occurred about March 1612 which focused attention on the stories of witchcraft in the Forest and there is little doubt that Roger Nowell, a believer in witchcraft and a zealous supporter of the King's theories about witches, would do his utmost to substantiate the rumours.

An examination of the proceedings at various Courts under Roger Nowell will show how an almost casual enquiry into the activities of Demdike eventually resulted in the imprisonment of thirteen persons on a charge of witchcraft.

March 13th 1612.

At some time about the beginning of March 1612, (*See Footnote*), Bessie Whittle, daughter of Chattox of West Close broke into the "fire-house" of Malkin Tower and carried away "all or most of their linen clothes, half a peck of cut oatmeal and a quantity of meal, all worth twenty shilling and more". On the following Sunday, Alizon Davies saw Bessie wearing "a band and coif", part of the stolen property, and soon afterwards reported the matter to the Greave of the Forest who then brought the matter to the notice of Roger Nowell, the local magistrate. As a result of the enquiry which was held at Read Hall on March 13th, Bessie Whittle was committed to Lancaster gaol. Richard Shuttleworth of Gawthorpe in April 1613 paid a rate of 6d. laid on him as a landowner in West Close "towards the bringing up (to Lancaster) of Bessie Chattock's clothes".

At Read Hall, one can imagine that Bessie would seek revenge by making accusations of witchcraft against Demdike, the leading member of the Malkin Tower household, and, as only Alizon Davies was present when the charges were made, on her depended the defence of her grandmother. Unfortunately, under the skilful questioning of Roger Nowell, awed by her surroundings and in the presence of a magistrate, and

This date is the only deviation from the records of Mr. Potts which the present writer has made. On March 30th 1612 Alizon Davies gave evidence that the robbery by one of the Chattox family took place "eleven years ago" and in her next statement declared that her father had died "eleven years ago". Considering that Richard Shuttleworth paid part of the cost of sending "Bessie Chattock's clothes" to her in prison at Lancaster in 1613, it would appear that the dates in Alizon's evidence have been confused and that the robbery occurred not in 1601 but in the early part of 1612.

perhaps influenced by threats or promises of leniency, Alizon made four damning admissions:

1. Demdike had advised Alizon to become a witch.
2. Demdike had bewitched a cow which John Nutter of the Bullhole Farm had asked her to cure.
3. Demdike, while in bed, had once charmed a can of milk so that a quarter pound of butter appeared in it.
4. About 1610, Demdike had cursed Richard Baldwin of Wheethead and "after a year" a "woman child" of Richard Baldwin had died which Alizon thought was due to witchcraft. (Ellen, daughter of Richard Baldwin of Wheethead, was buried at Colne on September 8th 1610).

It is difficult to believe that Alizon willingly gave this information about her grandmother or that she really thought the statements to be true; she was most probably repeating the rumours of her neighbours. John Nutter would certainly not have invited Demdike to attend one of his cattle had he believed in the power of her reputed witchcraft which inevitably worked for evil, nor did he ever accuse Demdike of causing his loss. As for the case of murder by witchcraft at Wheethead, there had undoubtedly been a bitter quarrel between Richard Baldwin and Demdike but though Baldwin's daughter fell sick the following morning and died a year later, no member of the Baldwin family was summoned to give evidence.

Possibly nothing more would have been heard officially of Pendle witchcraft if it had not been for the unfortunate event that occurred five days later.

March 18th 1612.

On this day, as Alizon was on her way to Trawden Forest to begin her normal occupation of begging, she met a pedlar, John Law of Halifax, near the present Colne Cemetery. When she asked him to sell her some pins he refused saying that he did not wish to have his pack stolen. (Another but untruthful report stated that the pedlar gave her some pins because she had no money.) Alizon, doubtless weary with her long walk and in no good frame of mind, cursed him for his meanness and then, most unfortunately, within a few minutes after they had parted, the pedlar had a seizure. He was carried to an alehouse in Colne where he was visited, probably the same day, by Alizon who "staid not long there, but looked on him and went

9

away". Here was a matter for further investigation by Roger Nowell; at last, he had a recent case of apparent witchcraft, based on actual fact.

March 21st 1612.

Abraham Law went to see his father at Colne and found him unable to speak and with "his left side lamed all save his eye". Later the unfortunate man partially recovered his speech and complained that "he was pricked with knives, elsons (awls or bodkins) and sickles" and that "the hurt he had in his lameness was done by witchcraft by Alizon Davies".

March 29th 1612.

Abraham Law brought Alizon to see his father who accused her of having bewitched him. Alizon confessed and on her knees asked the pedlar for forgiveness, "whereupon the father did forgive her".

Was Alizon Davies really convinced in her own mind that she was a witch able to maim and kill? Surely she was the victim of her environment and circumstances. Living in wretched poverty with a blind old grandmother, a badly disfigured mother and a subnormal brother, earning a living by begging, listening to the curses and dire threats shouted by her people when help was refused, and well knowing the ugly rumours in the neighbour-hood about the evil practices at Malkin Tower, Alizon herself must have been doubtful about herself and her powers, if any. When the pedlar collapsed some two hundred yards away, her first reaction must have been one of shock and astonishment that a curse which she had doubtless made very many times before should, on this occasion, be so quickly and realistically fulfilled. Then terror and fear filled her mind and drove her to look at the sick man as he lay in Colne, hoping against hope that he was not so ill as had been thought. Finally, ignorant, terror stricken and unconsciously moulded by the character of her home life, Alizon probably decided that she was really a witch and that her curse had really maimed a man; she had neither pride nor joy in the apparent possession of such an unsolicited evil power and begged forgiveness from her victim.

March 30th 1612.

Alizon Davies with her mother Elizabeth and her brother James appeared at Read Hall on a summons to be examined by a magistrate. In the presence of Authority in the person of Roger Nowell, Alizon would be too awed and too frightened to do anything but agree with the suggestions implied in the magistrate's questions. Her depositions sealed her fate at her later trial at Lancaster for she confessed that she had sold her soul to the Devil in the shape of a black dog when she was walking towards "the Rough Lee" and that the dog had next appeared on March 18th when she told it to "lame" the pedlar because he suggested she was a thief. This was apparently a full confession of all her activities and she must have been considerably surprised when her brother James, doubtless under further promptings from the magistrate, stated that she had confessed to bewitching a child of Henry Bulcock; no further enquiries were made into the truth of this new allegation.

The only statement that could be obtained from Elizabeth Davies was to the effect that her mother Demdike had "had a place on her left side by the space of forty years". She possibly tried to insist that "the place" was a natural mark on her mother's body, but in the view of Roger Nowell it was the mark left by the Devil when he sucked her blood. It is rather remarkable that there is no mention of any enquiry about the Devil's mark in the case of many others of the so-called witches, since a mark was regarded as a sure proof that a person was a witch; none of them apparently had a mark except Demdike though Alizon did admit that after she surrendered to the black dog she had a blue mark for six months. Apparently in 1612 the absence of a mark was not regarded as significant or proof of innocence; in 1633 three local women were acquitted on the charge of witchcraft and, among other things, it was stated that they had no witch marks.

When answering the magistrate's questions about Chattox, Alizon felt no constraint for she could bring up not only the old rumours about the evil practices of the old witch of West Close but could invent new ones; moreover, she could get revenge for the accusations made on March 13th by Bessie Chattox against Demdike. In fact, she accused Chattox of murdering four men, killing a cow, despoiling ale and charming milk. In her statements, Alizon maintained that her own father, who had died eleven years previously, was bewitched by Chattox because he failed to keep up his yearly payment to her of a small quantity of meal; that two years ago, Anne Nutter, daughter of Anthony Nutter of Newchurch, was bewitched by Chattox and died after three weeks because she was annoyed to see Anne and Alizon laughing together in the Nutter's home; that two years previously when John Moore of Higham complained that Chattox had bewitched his drink, she bewitched his child which died after six months; that six or seven years before when Hugh Moore of Pendle complained that Chattox had bewitched his cattle, she caused him to die after six months saying "Chattox has bewitched me"; and finally, that when Elizabeth Redfern begged a dishful of milk from the Bullhole Farm, her mother Chattox charmed it with two sticks across the can but the farmer's son was so annoyed that he kicked the can over "wherefore one of the cows died after three or four days".

Here was much material to be investigated by the magistrate but it is strange that Alizon did not report the rumours about the eighteen-year-old deaths of the two Nutters of Greenhead, which were ascribed to the witchcraft of Chattox. Roger Nowell now decided that the best thing to do was to bring the two protagonists, Demdike and Chattox, face to face before him.

April 2nd 1612.

On this day, Demdike, Chattox and Anne Redfern appeared for examination before the magistrate in Fence. It is uncertain whether he used threats of punishment or promises of pardon or relied on the tendency among some old people to revel in boastful exaggeration, but, aided by superstitious witnesses who were either frightened or revengeful, Nowell did secure damning confessions from the two blind old women of eighty; Anne Redfern, a more level headed person, steadily refused to make a confession or implicate anyone in the general charge.

Demdike admitted that twenty years previously as she was coming home from begging she met near a stonepit in Goldshaw (Newchurch) a spirit or devil in the shape of a boy wearing a black and brown coat. He said his name was "Tibb". Though she then gave her soul to him, she made no use of his proffered help for five or six years, at the end of which he came to her as a brown dog and sucked her blood; at the time she was asleep, wearing only a smock, and nursing a child on her knee but she could only cry "Jesus save my child" and was too frightened to say "Jesus save me". Questioned about the death of Richard Baldwin's child, she related that "a little before Christmas last", i.e. December 1611, since Richard Baldwin had not paid the wages due to her daughter Elizabeth for working a few days for him, she, being blind, was taken by her granddaughter Alizon to ask about them and that they were met by Baldwin near his house with the words "Get out of my ground, whores and witches; I will burn the one of you and hang the other". Tibb then appeared and was told "Revenge thee either of him or his". (Alizon had previously stated on March 13th that the whole affair took place "two or three years ago" and that Baldwin's daughter was taken ill on the morning after the quarrel and died after some months—actually in September 1610. Demdike, whose memory must have been failing, stated the quarrel had taken place only five months earlier, in December 1611).

Demdike's confession does not definitely show what means were used to fulfil the curse, but one infers from her description of killing by "Pictures (images) of Clay" that Baldwin's daughter was supposedly killed by such a method. "The speediest way to take away a man's life by Witchcraft is to make a Picture of Clay like unto the shape of the person they mean to kill and dry it thoroughly; and when they would have them to be ill in any one place more than another, then take a Thorn or Pin and prick it into that part of the Picture you would so have to be ill; and when you would have any part of the Body to consume away, then take that part of the Picture and burn it. And when they would have the whole body to consume away, then take the remnant of the said Picture and burn it; and so thereupon by that means, the body shall die".

Several witnesses were prepared to swear that Chattox and her daughter, Anne Redfern, practised the arts of witchcraft.

1. James Robinson alleged that, six years before, Chattox came to his house on a certain Friday, Saturday and Monday to help his wife with carding wool and that after she had dipped her cup on several occasions in some freshly brewed ale to get a drink, their ale for the next eight or nine weeks·was spoiled. More important accusations concerned the Nutters of Greenhead, landlords of the cottage in West Close where Chattox and her daughters lived.

13

Robert Nutter (bur. in Burnley 1613?) m. Elizabeth —
|
Christopher (bur. in Burnley 1593)
┌─────────────────────┴──────────┬──────────────────┐
Robert (bur. in Burnley 1595)   John   Margaret (born
                                          1568) m. — Crook

The same witness affirmed that in 1594 he was living at Greenhead (probably as a servant) when the younger Robert Nutter
cómplained of a sickness caused by Chattox and Redfern and
that shortly afterwards when the same Robert was about to set
out for Chester with Sir Richard Shuttleworth he told Thomas
Redfern that on his return he would persuade his father to evict
the Redferns and Chattox from their cottage; this was not done
because Robert died in Cheshire on his way home (1595).

2. John Nutter alleged that eighteen or nineteen years previously (1594 or 1593) when he was walking home at Christmas
from Burnley with his brother Robert and his father Christopher, Robert declared that he had been bewitched by Chattox
and Anne Redfern and begged the father to "cause them to be laid
in Lancaster Gaol" but the father told him he was a "foolish lad".

3. Margaret Crook stated that, after a quarrel between her
brother Robert Nutter and Anne Redfern, Robert was taken
ill and said "a hundred times at the least" that Anne Redfern
and her associates had bewitched him to death. Margaret
further stated that her father, Christopher Nutter, was ill for
several months before he died (in 1593) and said many times
that he was bewitched but he would name no one responsible.

4. Demdike contributed to the general attack on Chattox and
Redfern by stating that six months before the death of Robert
Nutter (1595) she had seen them on either side of a ditch three
yards from the east end of their house in West Close with two
complete images in clay and a third one in process of making.
Tibb, who was with her in the shape of a black cat, urged her
to make others and told her they were the "pictures" of
Christopher Nutter, Robert Nutter and Mary, his wife; when
she refused, Tibb pushed her into the ditch shedding the milk
she was carrying and then disappeared only to reappear again
in the shape of a hare to accompany her for a quarter of a mile,
though she refused to say anything to it. From the depositions
of Demdike it would appear that she considered her own
fictitious adventures quite as important as those of Chattox.
Tibb's knowledge of dates and events must have been faulty
since Christopher Nutter in 1595 had been dead for two years.

Chattox, decrepit, nearly blind, eighty years of age and probably failing in mind, was now ready with the help of the magistrate and witnesses to make a complete and full confession. She informed Nowell that fourteen or fifteen years previously "a Thing like a Christian man" had come to her and at various times during the next four years had asked for her soul and that at last "in her own house" she had granted his request on the promise that she should not lack anything and would get any revenge she desired; the Spirit or Devil ordered her to call him by the name of "Fancy". Possibly invited by the magistrate to say what she knew about Richard Baldwin, and vaguely remembering that something had once happened to him, Chattox affirmed that Fancy had once wanted to hurt the wife of Richard Baldwin of Pendle but as she would not agree, the Spirit, still in the likeness of a man, tried to bite her arm. If Richard Baldwin of Pendle is the same as Richard Baldwin of Wheethead, then he must have been in an unenviable position for both Tibb and Fancy were determined to do him an injury. As far as the Nutters of Greenhead were concerned, Chattox stated that before 1595, when Robert Nutter the younger died, his grandmother Elizabeth requested her (Chattox), "Lomeshaye wife" of Burnley and Jane Boothman of Burnley to kill young Robert Nutter so that the land might go to a collateral branch of the family; Thomas Redfern, son in law of Chattox, persuaded her to have nothing to do with the plot and presented a capon to the late schoolmaster of Colne, Mr. Nicholas Baldwin of Greenfield (died 1610) for using his learning to "stay" "Lomeshaye wife". However, Chattox admitted that the three of them later did all they could to kill young Robert Nutter. (Jane Boothman had an illegitimate child in 1571; "Lomeshaye wife" was the wife of John Hargreaves nicknamed "Lomeshaye" and probably lived at Heyhead, Brierfield; she was buried in Burnley on March 5th 1612, a few days before the enquiry into witchcraft was opened.) Young Robert Nutter and the Chattox family later quarrelled because he made improper overtures to Anne Redfern who indignantly rejected his suggestions so that when he left the house in great anger he shouted "If ever the ground came to him, she should never dwell on his land". Chattox then related how Fancy in the likeness of a man had come to her in the Laund and had been told to revenge her "whereupon the said Robert Nutter lived about a quarter of a year and then died".

15

Discrepancies in the depositions of witnesses and confessions of the so-called witches will be discussed later but here it may be pointed out that Chattox several times maintained that she first met Fancy "fourteen or fifteen years" previously, i.e. 1598 or 1597, and that she gave her soul to him after four years, i.e. in 1602 or 1601, but she also claimed to have been responsible for the death of Robert Nutter which occurred in 1595 and to have made even an earlier attempt on his life.

Other cases of witchcraft in which Chattox claimed the major share were comparatively unimportant: 1. She had been asked by John Moore's wife to amend some sour ale and had tried to do so by reciting a charm but unfortunately the lady was much annoyed that witchcraft had been used. Fancy was therefore told to bite the head of one of Moore's cows and make it "go mad"; the cow died six weeks later. 2. She had told Fancy to kill a cow belonging to Anthony Nutter because he was friendly with the Demdike family. The accusation made by Alizon Davies was that Chattox had bewitched to death Anne Nutter for the same reason.

Chattox completed her confession with the interesting information that the Devil or Fancy had taken most of her sight, that he sometimes came in the likeness of a gaping bear and that the last time she saw him was "upon Thursday last year but one next before Midsummer day in the evening like a bear" when he pulled her down because she would not speak to him.

On the evidence and confessions thus obtained, Roger Nowell committed Demdike, Chattox, Alizon Davies and Anne Redfern to Lancaster Gaol to await trial at the August Assize.

Good Friday, April 6th 1612.

On Good Friday and less than a week after the four Pendle Forest women had been lodged in Lancaster Castle, several friends of the Demdike family visited Malkin Tower. Two of the visitors were relatives, two were near neighbours, some went out of idle curiosity to talk and discuss possible verdicts at the forthcoming trial in August, while one at any rate went out of a pure desire to be of some help to the stricken family. When rumours of what had happened at Malkin Tower reached Read Hall, Nowell decided that more enquiries should be made. His examination of Elizabeth Davies and her children James and Jenet convinced him that Demdike's old home had been the scene of a witches' coven and that all who had been present must be witches.

April 27th 1612.

The enquiry was held at the house of James Wilsey before Roger Nowell and another magistrate, Nicholas Bannister of Altham. They first concentrated their attention on the Good Friday meeting at Malkin Tower to determine why it was held, what happened there and who was present. The magistrates must have been sorely disappointed that the meeting was so prosaic, though Mr. Potts would have us believe that "they met, according to solemn appointment, solemnised this great Festival Day according to their formal order with great cheer, merry company and much conference". The clerk's description was imaginative for there was apparently no dancing, no orgies, and neither address nor sermon from the Devil; nor was there any delicacy to whet the appetites of the persons present, no toads and no flesh from corpses; all that was provided was beef, bacon and roast mutton.

Knowing well from experience gained on March 30th that Elizabeth Davies was reluctant to give evidence, Nowell first examined her son James who, being mentally sub-normal, would be most likely to make incriminating statements.

James affirmed with evident truth that he had stolen a sheep from John Robinson of Barley and had killed it at Malkin Tower to provide for a dinner about noon on Good Friday for a number of persons, whereof three were men. They included
The wife of Hugh Hargreaves of Barley
Jane, wife of Christopher Bulcock, and John, her son, both of Moss End
Alice Nutter of Roughlee
Christopher Holgate and his wife, Elizabeth
Elizabeth, wife of Christopher Hargreaves of Thorney-holme
Alice Gray of Colne
Mouldheel's wife (Katherine Hewitt) of Colne
Elizabeth Davies (his mother) and himself.
He asserted that he did not know the names of the other people present.

The same witness said that his mother had told him that the witches had met for three reasons:

(*a*) To name the Spirit or Familiar of his sister, Alizon; this could not be done as Alizon was in prison and could not be present. Such a proposal was certainly curious since Tibb, Fancy and Dandy had themselves told the witches what they should be called. If James meant to imply that they had met to rebaptise Alizon in the name of the Devil, it is remarkable that such a ceremony had been so long deferred since according to his own testimony Alizon had been a witch for a year.

(*b*) To liberate the four women from gaol by killing the gaoler and blowing up the Castle. James said that he heard the witches talking about this scheme but one imagines that they were merely expressing a far fetched hope that it might be possible.

(*c*) To help Preston's wife of Gisburn Parish to kill Mr. Lister of Westby because he had borne malice against her and "her power was not strong enough to do it herself, being now less than beforetime it had been".

We have no account of what actually happened at the meeting but a vivid description of the dispersal of the witches was given by James Davies—"all the witches went out of the house in their shapes and likenesses. And they all, by that they were forth of the doors, were gotten on horseback, like unto foals, some of one colour, some of another; and Preston's wife was the last; and when she got on horseback, they all presently vanished out of sight". James also tells us that before separating they all agreed to meet at Preston's wife's house on Good Friday 1613 but that if necessity arose warning would be given that they should gather on Rumbles Moor.

Elizabeth Davies gave evidence that the persons who dined at Malkin Tower on Good Friday were witches and that their names were as given by her son, James. She agreed that they had met about "The Christening of the Spirit" and the killing of Mr. Lister but she did not remember that they ever talked of killing the gaoler, blowing up the Castle and releasing the prisoners. She admitted that other witches present were two women of Burnley Parish "whose names Alice Nutter knew" and Anne Cronkshaw of Marsden.

The evidence of Jenet Davies, a pert girl of nine, closely followed the statements made by her brother. She asserted that about twenty persons, whereof only two were men, dined at Malkin Tower and that, according to her mother's information, they were all witches. She knew the names of six witches who were present: the wife of Hugh Hargreaves; Christopher Holgate, her uncle; Alice Nutter of Roughlee; Christopher Hargreaves of Thorneyholme and his wife; the rest of the company she did not know except that her mother and brother were there. Jenet included Christopher Hargreaves, not given by her brother, but it is strange that she did not mention the Bulcocks who lived at Moss End, less than half a mile from Malkin Tower. In the following August she could remember that John Bulcock had turned the spit to roast the mutton for the meal at Malkin Tower.

Further examination of James Davies and his mother about their own activities brought more astounding revelations and "confessions".

James Davies stated that two years previously, i.e. 1610, on the Thursday before Easter, his grandmother told him to go to Communion at Church but not to eat the bread but give it to "a Thing" that should meet him on the way homewards; in spite of the injunction, he did eat the bread and was threatened two hundred and twenty yards distant from the Church by "a Thing in the shape of a hare" because he could not offer it the consecrated bread. Then, courageously, "he marked himself to God" and the Thing vanished. Before the following Easter Monday he met near Newchurch "a Thing like a black dog" which asked him for his soul and promised "revenge" but he replied that "his soul belonged to Saviour Jesus Christ" though he was ready to surrender the rest of himself. Apparently he was then a witch with a Spirit that was to be called "Dandy". In Easter week he had a wordy quarrel with Mrs. Townley of Carr Hall who accused him and his mother of stealing turves and drove him away from the housedoor, whereupon Dandy appeared and told him to make a clay image of Mrs. Townley. He followed the instructions the next morning, dried the clay image at night and crumbled it all away during the week; two days later, Mrs. Townley was dead. Unfortunately for the truth of the details of the story, Mrs. Townley died a day or two before October 25th 1611, some eighteen months after the making of the image. James also admitted that by the help of Dandy he had killed John Duckworth of the Laund because he refused to carry out a promise to give him an old shirt.

Mr. Potts has not recorded the full confession of Elizabeth Davies perhaps because parts of it were too obscene for publication. She admitted to having a Spirit named "Ball" which appeared to her as a brown dog and that in 1608 because John

Robinson of Barley had accused her of having an illegitimate child (Jenet??) she had made a picture of clay at the west end of Malkin Tower, dried it by a fire and then crumbled it; within a week, Robinson had died. She also confessed that she, her mother Demdike, and Alice Nutter had joined forces to bewitch and kill Henry Mitton.

Having elicited some information about the events on Good Friday at Malkin Tower and having secured two more "confessions", Nowell felt it his duty to interrogate the witnesses present about the other witches.

Re Alice Nutter of Roughlee.

James Davies said his grandmother had told him that she, Elizabeth Davies and Alice Nutter had killed Henry Mitton of "the Roughlee" by witchcraft because he would not give her a penny. Elizabeth Davies confessed her part in the death of Mitton and added that Alice Nutter knew two women from Burnley Parish who had dinner at Malkin Tower on Good Friday. The only named women of Burnley Parish were "Lomeshaye wife" and Jane Boothman; of these, the first was dead before the Good Friday meeting.

Re Jane Bulcock and her son, John, both of Moss End, Newchurch.

James Davies stated that they had been at Malkin Tower and had confessed to bewitching at Newfield Edge a woman named Jenet, wife of John Dean and making her lose her reason and that they had agreed to help Jenet Preston with the murder of Mr. Lister and Leonard Lister. Elizabeth Davies added that Jane Bulcock knew the names of some witches about Padiham and Burnley and that John Bulcock had agreed to the murder of Mr. Lister.

Re Katherine Hewitt (Mouldheel's wife) and Alice Gray, both of Colne.

James Davies said that both of them had been at Malkin Tower on Good Friday and that they had confessed to murdering "Fould's wife child Ann" and to having under their control a child of Michael Hartley's of Colne. (Ann, daughter of Nicholas Foulds was buried at Colne on July

4th 1607). Elizabeth Davies agreed with the evidence of her son and added that Katherine Hewitt had covenanted with Jenet Preston to murder Mr. Lister.

Re Demdike, Chattox and Anne Redfern.

James was much more imaginative when he described the witchcraft of the more notorious of the witches. He asserted that about a month previously as he was going home to Malkin Tower in the evening, he met a brown dog coming away from the house some fifty to sixty yards distant; that two or three nights later when he was the same distance from home he heard children "scriking and crying"; that about five days later and at a distance of less than a hundred yards from Malkin Tower he heard a "foul yelling" like unto a great number of cats; and that three nights later at midnight a "thing" black in colour and of the size of a hare or cat lay heavy on him for an hour and then jumped out of the bedroom window.

His powers of imagination increased when he spoke of Chattox and Anne Redfern. He asserted that Chattox had told him how she had attended a funeral at Newchurch in 1600 and had taken three skulls which had been thrown out of a grave and that she had taken eight teeth, four of which she kept and four she gave to Demdike. To impress the magistrates with the truth of his story, he produced for their inspection four teeth which he said were those given to Demdike and which he and Henry Hargreaves of Goldshaw, constable of the Forest, had found buried at a depth of half a yard at the west end of Malkin Tower; he also added that with the teeth was a crumbled clay image of Anne, daughter of Anthony Nutter.

When questioned about Anne Redfern, he said that two years previously he had seen three images, half a yard in size, at the end of Redfern's house; Mr. Redfern himself held one, his daughter Mary held a second and Anne Redfern had one which was crumbling but he could not say whose image it was; after leaving them and going some fifty or sixty yards, "a thing" like a hare appeared and spit fire at him.

Re Jenet Preston of Gisburn.

James Davies repeated the statements he had made

previously about the reasons for the Good Friday meeting and once more described how the witches had dispersed. He added that Jenet Preston had brought her Spirit with her in the shape of a white foal and that since Good Friday he had been taken by Henry Hargreaves to Gisburn and had there identified Jenet Preston as the person present at Malkin Tower.

As a result of the enquiry held on April 27th 1612 the following persons were committed to Lancaster Castle to await trial with the four women already imprisoned there :-

Elizabeth Davies

James Davies

Alice Nutter

Katherine Hewitt

Alice Gray

John Bulcock

Jane Bulcock

(Jenet Preston of Gisburn was committed to York Castle)

Much of the evidence given by witnesses was undoubtedly based on rumours which inevitably varied not only in details but in the most important facts. Some discrepancies in the depositions have already been noticed but the most glaring inconsistencies may be seen in the statements regarding the death of Anne, daughter of Anthony Nutter, and in the evidence concerning John Moore. In the first case, Alizon Davies maintained on March 30th that because she and Anne Nutter had laughed at Chattox who was passing the Nutter's house, the old woman had cursed Anne so that on the following day the girl fell sick and died within three weeks: Chattox however gave evidence that her Spirit had killed only a cow belonging to Anthony Nutter because his family was friendly with the Demdike clan: on April 27th James Davies said he had found a crumbled image of Anne Nutter outside Malkin Tower, implying that it was Demdike who was responsible for the death of the girl. In the evidence about John Moore, Alizon Davies stated that Chattox had bewitched the drink of John Moore and that she heard Chattox say that she "would meet with John Moore or his" and that John Moore's child then fell sick, languished for six months and then died; she added more details that she had seen Chattox sitting in her own garden with an image of clay "like unto a child" in her apron which was used to hide the image and that her mother thought it was "the picture of John Moore's child". The version given by Chattox of the same affair was that she had been sent for by John Moore's wife "to help drink that was bewitched" and that after she had amended the drink by reciting a charm, Moore's wife was "grieved at her"; thereupon she had called Fancy and bade him bite a brown cow by the head and make the cow go mad so that "the cow went mad accordingly and died within six weeks next after or thereabouts".

Probably on account of her advanced age, Demdike was unable to endure for long the harships of life in a dark, airless and overcrowded cell and she mercifully died before her trial. Perhaps because the governor of the prison feared that other prisoners might die before the coming of the Judges and so cheat the country of an exciting story of witchcraft, the Authorities at Lancaster decided to interrogate further both Chattox and James Davies.

May 19th 1612

The examiners were William Sands, Mayor of Lancaster; James Anderton of Clayton, J.P.; and Thomas Covell, Governor of the Prison.

Chattox said that fourteen years previously i.e. 1598 she had been persuaded by Demdike to become a witch and that the Devil came to her about midnight at Malkin Tower in the likeness of a man and that she then consented to allow the Devil to suck her blood. (On April 2nd Chattox said she gave her soul to the Devil "in her own house"). At the same time a spotted dog came to Demdike and promised "gold, silver and worldly wealth", provided them with "flesh, butter, cheese, bread and drink" and "gave light though there was neither fire nor candle light". After they had eaten, Tibb and Fancy carried away the remnants but she admitted that though they ate, "they were never the fuller". She stated that she, Demdike and Widow Lomeshaye had bewitched Robert Nutter and added a new allegation that Demdike had bewitched to death Richard Assheton, son of Richard Assheton of Downham.

James Davies stated that when he told Dandy that he would give that part of himself which was his own to give, the Devil insisted that he was above Jesus Christ and once more de-

23

manded his soul. James maintained that he still refused to submit and finally on the Tuesday before being committed to Lancaster when he again refused the Devil's demands, Dandy left him "giving a most fearful cry and yell and at the same time caused a great flash of fire to show about him"; after that, the Spirit did not again come to him.

August 9th 1612

On this day Nicholas Bannister held an enquiry into the rumours of witchcraft as practised by Margaret Pearson of Padiham. There must have been some unrecorded evidence that Margaret had bewitched a mare belonging to a man named Dodgeon but the only available evidence against Margaret at the time was produced by Jenet Booth who stated that when she boiled a pan of milk in the Pearson's home she found a toad, or something very like a toad, in the fire under the pan; Margaret carried the toad out of doors but what became of it the witness did not know. Margaret Pearson was committed to Lancaster to await trial for witchcraft.

July 27th 1612. Trial of Jenet Preston at York.

Jenet Preston was arraigned before Judge Altham on a charge of killing by witchcraft Mr. Thomas Lister and of causing great loss to Mr. Leonard Lister. In 1611 she had been before the Assize Court for the murder of a child but had been found not guilty and acquitted. At her present trial the depositions of James, Elizabeth and Jenet Davies were read out to show that at Malkin Tower she had enlisted the help of her friends from Pendle Forest to kill Mr. Lister, but the most important evidence, in the opinion of Mr. Potts, was provided by a witness who stated that when the prisoner was brought before the dead body of Mr. Thomas Lister "the corpse bled fresh blood when she touched it". She was found guilty and executed at York Castle.

August 17th, 18th and 19th 1612. The Trial at Lancaster.

The Lancaster Assize Court opened with pomp and ceremony on Monday, August 17th, and with Judge Bromley playing the leading role. With him on the Bench was Judge Altham and, to assist them in their deliberations, several important personalities including Lord Gerard and Sir Richard Hoghton. The prosecution lay in the hands of Roger Nowell who had made the preliminary examinations and had sent the accused for trial; the Clerk of the Court was Mr. Thomas Potts of London. The prisoners, frightened, suffering from the foul conditions of prison life and now crowded together and guarded by gaolers, had no counsel to plead for them nor were they allowed to call witnesses to speak on their behalf. All that they could now do was to plead "Guilty" or "Not Guilty", listen to the evidence of witnesses against them, hear their own "confessions" and depositions read out against them, answer questions, and then wait for the inevitable verdict. The Judges, if they were so disposed, might ask questions to help the accused, but it will be seen what use was made of this rule in the case of the Pendle Witches.

Monday, August 17th 1612.

Anne Whittle nicknamed Chattox was the first to be called and was charged with practising witchcraft on Robert Nutter of Greenhead and slaying him. She pleaded "Not Guilty". Nowell then read out her "voluntary confession" of April 2nd and the evidences of Alizon Davies of March 30th and of Demdike, James Davies and James Robinson of April 2nd. From the remarks of Mr. Potts, one may infer that other witnesses were called and other evidence produced against the prisoner but, in his opinion, the most important part of the prosecution's case was her confession. Mr. Potts also tells us that "in her examination and confession she always dealt very plainly and truly; for upon a special occasion, being examined in open Court, she was never found to vary, but always to agree in one and the self same thing". On the other hand, the confessions vary considerably and often contradict the evidence of witnesses; in fact, on her own confession she could not have been a witch at the time of the death of Robert Nutter, with whose death she was charged.

Mr. Potts also writes of "her great contrition and repentance after she was committed to the Castle at Lancaster" and states that at the end of her trial "with weeping tears she humbly acknowledged them to be true and cried unto God

25

for Mercy and forgiveness of her sins and humbly prayed my Lord (Bromley) to be merciful unto Anne Redfern her daughter". One can well imagine this poverty stricken, partially blind, and mentally unstable old woman of eighty, who perhaps had traded on her reputation as a witch to earn a living, was suddenly shocked at the trial into an unaccustomed clearness of mind and, realising her own hopeless position, prayed for leniency not for herself but for her daughter.

Elizabeth Davies, daughter of the deceased Demdike, was then called and charged with killing by witchcraft John Robinson nicknamed "Swyer", James Robinson and (jointly with others) Henry Mitton. She pleaded "Not Guilty". Nowell then read out her confession of April 27th and the evidence of her children, James and Jenet, of the same date. The mother lost all control of herself, shrieked curses, cried out against her children and would confess nothing. The appearance of Jenet as a witness against her roused still more curses so that she had to be removed from the Court. The Judge then ordered Jenet "the maid to be set upon a table in the presence of the whole Court who delivered her evidence in that honorable assembly". She declared her mother was a witch and that with the help of Ball had killed John and James Robinson and Henry Mitton. At the end of her trial, Elizabeth Davies was brought back again into Court; she persisted in her refusal to confess to the charges against her but cried for mercy.

Elizabeth Davies, like so many who have been handicapped from birth by a physical deformity, probably felt a grudge against everyone. She was ignorant, uncouth, unloving and unloveable, and subject to outbursts of violence. Moody and taciturn, in the few cases where she reluctantly gave evidence, there is no display of imagination, no vivid description of her Spirit; she merely agreed with the statements given by others and, if she volunteered information, it was almost second hand e.g. "Alice Nutter knows two witches in Burnley" and "Jane Bulcock knows witches about Padiham". As a daughter of Demdike and being abnormal, both physically and mentally, she would easily earn an unfounded reputation for witchcraft.

James Davies, who had been reared in the countryside, had suffered in health from his confinement in prison and was "insensible weak and unable in all things as he could neither speak, hear or stand but was held up when he was brought to the place of trial". He pleaded "Not Guilty" to charges of killing Anne Townley of Carr Hall and James Duckworth of

26

the Laund. Mr. Henry Townley was called to give evidence but Mr. Potts has not recorded it. The prosecutor read out the depositions of the prisoner made on April 27th and then called on the ever willing Jenet, of whom Mr. Potts writes "It was wonderful to the Court in so great a Presence and Audience, with what modesty, government and understanding she delivered that evidence against the prisoner at the Bar, being her own natural brother". In her evidence she stated that her brother had been a witch for three years and had a Spirit called "Dandy" which had advised on the killing of Mrs. Townley and that shortly afterwards she herself had seen the lady "nothing well" in her kitchen at Carr Hall. James also pleaded "Not Guilty" to the charges of killing by witchcraft John Hargreaves of Goldshaw Booth and Blaize Hargreaves of Higham, which he "slenderly denied and thereupon insisted". Jenet again gave evidence on the new indictments and stated that her brother had killed the two Hargreaves. Other witnesses were called and depositions made on April 27th were read though they had nothing to do with the charges except that the prisoner had been present in his own home on Good Friday and was therefore presumably a witch.

James Davies was obviously mentally unbalanced, inclined to be brutish and quickly frightened into saying anything that he thought would please his examiners at Read Hall. His childish mind could easily imagine the unnatural and the impossible and, as part of his childish boasting, could talk of his challenge to the Devil to take his soul.

On the evening of Monday, August 17th, Chattox, Elizabeth Davies and James Davies were found guilty of committing the offences named in the indictments.

Tuesday, August 18th 1612.

Late in the afternoon, Anne Redfern was indicted for the murder (1595) of Robert Nutter of Greenhead but as the evidence against her was "not very pregnant" (satisfactory), she was acquitted by the jury on this charge.

Wednesday, August 19th 1612.

Anne Redfern was charged with the murder (1593) of Christopher Nutter, father of Robert, and pleaded "Not

Guilty" (much to the annoyance of Mr. Potts). Three depositions of April 2nd and one of April 27th were read,— (a) Demdike stated that Chattox and Anne Redfern had made three images of the Nutter family, including Christopher, (b) Margaret Crook said her father Christopher Nutter had declared he was bewitched but that he would name no one responsible, (c) John Nutter said that his father Christopher had called his brother Robert a fool for imagining that he had been bewitched, (d) James Davies asserted that the Chattox family had made three images of clay but "he could not tell whose picture it was". Other witnesses were called but their evidence was apparently too unimportant to be recorded. If the evidence against Anne Redfern for the murder of Robert Nutter was unsound or insufficient, then surely on the evidence before the jury she should have been acquitted on the charge of murdering Christopher Nutter. She made no so-called "confession" nor did she give any evidence against the other prisoners. Mr. Potts regretted that "no means could move her to repentance" but apparently he never considered the possibility that she might be completely innocent and therefore had no reason to be penitent.

Alice Nutter was then charged with the murder of Henry Mitton and pleaded "Not Guilty". She had made no confession at Read Hall and had not given any evidence of any sort; now, at her final trial at Lancaster, she steadily refused to say anything. The depositions of James and Elizabeth Davies of April 27th were read out stating that the prisoner had been present at Malkin Tower and that she with Demdike and Elizabeth Davies had killed Henry Mitton because he would not give a penny to Demdike. Jenet was again called upon for evidence and was asked by the Judge to pick out Alice Nutter from a group of prisoners. This was naturally a simple matter since she must have known the prisoner by sight from very early years. In order to trap Jenet, the Judge then asked her if she knew "Johan a Style" and Jenet replied that she had never heard of him; if he had asked about "Dick o' Miles", the young girl would have had to consider her answer. (It is obvious that neither Judge Bromley nor Mr. Potts recognised the meaning of such a name as "Dick o' Miles" which to their untutored London ears would sound like "Dick a Miles"). Potts states that Alice Nutter's "own children were never able to move her to confess any particular offence or declare anything even when about to die".

The presence of Alice Nutter amongst the so-called witches presents a great problem since she was far different in birth, upbringing and education from the rest of the prisoners. It was stated that "she was a rich woman; had a great estate and children of good hope" and was "of good temper, free from envy and malice". The theory that she and Nowell had quarrelled about the issue of a lawsuit cannot be substantiated. That she did call at Malkin Tower on Good Friday is quite possible but if so, the visit must have been for the purpose of helping the family. Pendle Forest was a stronghold of Roman Catholicism and many of the Nutters were of that Faith; in fact, two of them were executed as Jesuit priests, one in 1584 and the other in 1600. Alice Nutter may therefore have been on her way to a Catholic service which was illegal at that period and any confession that she had "called" at Malkin Tower would have inevitably led to questions as to where she was going. Any answer to that query would have started more questions about her Catholic friends and brought trouble to her co-religionists. The prisoner therefore remained silent. An old local legend has it that such was the reason for Alice Nutter being implicated in the affair of the Pendle Witches.

Katherine Hewitt was charged with the murder of Anne Foulds and pleaded "Not Guilty". After the depositions of James and Elizabeth Davies had been read, Jenet once again provided entertainment for the Court since, when asked to pick out the prisoner from many others she did so by taking her hand and telling the Court where the prisoner had sat at Malkin Tower; when questioned by the Judge whether "Joanne a Downe" was at the Feast, Jenet replied that no such woman was there.

At the end of the morning session of August 19th, the jury pronounced that Anne Redfern, Alice Nutter and Katherine Hewitt were guilty of the offences named in the indictments.

In the afternoon of August 19th, Jane Bulcock and her son, John, both of Moss End, Newchurch were indicted for be-witching Jenet Dean of Newfield Edge. Both pleaded "Not Guilty" and strenuously denied that they had ever been at Malkin Tower on Good Friday. Jenet however picked out Jane Bulcock (a near neighbour) from the prisoners as one of those present among the witches there and gave details of how John Bulcock had turned the spit to roast the stolen sheep. In her evidence of April 27th before Roger Nowell, Jenet had not mentioned the presence of the Bulcocks at the Feast.

The drama that was being enacted at Lancaster reached its height when Alizon Davies was arraigned on the charge of laming the pedlar, John Law. While surrounded by other prisoners, she fell on her knees and asked the Court to hear her; then being ordered to come forward, she knelt and confessed and asked for forgiveness. She admitted that she had been a witch from the time a black dog had sucked her blood "towards Roughlee", that it had appeared to her on March 18th when she told it to lame the pedlar, and finally that she had not seen it since March 23rd when she would not speak to it in a field near Newchurch. The pedlar himself appeared in Court to give the details of his illness and show the effects of Alizon's curse. All who were present pitied him and Alizon once again begged his forgiveness.

The jury then declared Jane and John Bulcock "Not Guilty" and Alizon Davies "Guilty" on her own confession. It is not quite clear why the jury refused to accept the testimonies of James and Jenet in the case of the Bulcocks but was willing to believe that they spoke the truth against the other prisoners.

Margaret Pearson of Padiham was the last to be called, charged with bewitching a mare belonging to one Dodgeon of Padiham; she pleaded "Not Guilty". On two previous occasions, Margaret had appeared for trial (a) for murder by witchcraft and (b) for bewitching a neighbour but had been acquitted on each charge. For the purpose of the present indictment, Chattox was brought back to give evidence and declared that Margaret Pearson had a Spirit in the likeness of a man with cloven hoofs, that she and the Spirit had entered Dodgeon's stable through a loophole and had sat on the mare, which later died, and finally that the prisoner had confessed to murdering by witchcraft the wife and daughter of a man named Childers. Jenet Booth's story about the toad in the hot fire at Pearson's house eventually convinced the jury that Margaret was guilty of killing the mare by witchcraft. She was sentenced to stand in the pillory on four market days at Clitheroe, Whalley, Padiham and Lancaster with a paper showing her offence and then to be imprisoned for one year in Lancaster gaol.

At the end of the trial, the Judge sentenced to death by hanging Anne Whittle (Chattox), Elizabeth Davies, James Davies, Alizon Davies, Anne Redfern, Alice Nutter, and Katherine Hewitt. The sentence was carried out in public, probably on the following day, August 20th. Alice Gray (whose trial is not recorded), John Bulcock and Jane Bulcock, who had been found "Not Guilty", were acquitted.

Thus ended the unromantic drama of the Pendle Witches. It seems to have begun almost casually on March 13th 1612 when Bessie Chattox, herself accused of theft, made accusations of witchcraft against Demdike, and Alizon Davies, shocked and frightened, gave four instances of her grandmother's evil practices. The second Act opened on March 18th when a pedlar's apoplectic seizure was linked with Alizon's curse on him for his meanness, was continued on March 30th with her tearful confession and vivid but revengeful charges of witchcraft against Chattox, and was concluded on April 2nd when Demdike, Chattox, Alizon Davies and Anne Redfern were committed for trial at the next Lancaster Assize. The next Act was carried out at Malkin Tower on Good Friday, April 6th, when several friends and relatives came to condole with the family, talk of what had happened and try to decide what was best to be done. The fourth Act was written by Roger Nowell who, as magistrate and witchhunter, trapped on April 27th all who had been present at the "witches' coven", except the pert and selfish Jenet. The final Act was carried through at Lancaster where the "witches" seem to have been taunted with their evil practices rather than proved guilty of performing them and where, a few hours after sentence was passed, most of them ended their days on the scaffold.

What truth can be found among the welter of idle tales and rumours, false confessions and lying evidence? In an age of superstition when belief in witchcraft was widespread, a suspicion became a rumour and then an indisputable fact so that it was almost inevitable that such characters as Demdike and Chattox, cunning, cruel, and living in dire poverty, should be regarded as witches. Possibly the two old women traded on their evil reputation to extort a living more easily from their frightened neighbours; possibly, too, they made images and recited charms to enhance their notoriety; to ascribe local deaths and injuries to their machinations was natural among superstitious people and apparently was not beyond the imagination of Nowell, Mr. Potts, the Judges and the Jury, but no prosecuting counsel of the present day would ever dream of bringing before a Court such a tissue of lies, rumours, uncorroborated statements and contradictory evidence.

With the exceptions of Alice Nutter and Anne Redfern, all the "witches" betrayed abnormalities. Demdike and Chattox,

31

the two distressed old women of eighty, were failing mentally but cunning enough to implicate each other in the crime of witchcraft and, with the ignorance and pride of old age, boasted of the powers they claimed to possess. The statements and evidence given by Demdike's daughter and grandchildren were consistent with their individual characters. Elizabeth Davies, soured in mind by her disfigurement, was taciturn and moody and reluctantly admitted only what other people had said; characteristically, she went into a frenzy of passion when she heard the lies spoken by her own children against her. Alizon, James and Jenet were, in modern parlance, "problem children". Alizon was frightened, credulous, ignorant and suffering from the ill effects of poverty and the character of her family; James was subnormal, vicious, incapable of work and had the imaginative mind of a child; he was prepared to embroider the figments of his imagination with as many details as Nowell was prepared to believe; Jenet was selfish, self-centred, and ready to say anything and agree with anything if only she could please the Court. With such people as Demdike, Chattox, Alizon, James and Jenet as witnesses, the magistrate would have little difficulty in getting answers to his questions that would inevitably lead them to the scaffold. The main statements on which one can rely as being true are that Demdike quarrelled with Richard Baldwin, that Chattox quarrelled with Robert Nutter, that Chattox was jealous of Anne Nutter's friendship with Demdike's granddaughter, that there was some sort of a gathering at Malkin Tower on Good Friday, that several local deaths, injuries and losses were erroneously thought to be the work of witches and that thirteen persons were sent for trial for witchcraft, of whom three were acquitted, one died in prison, one was punished in the pillory and by imprisonment and eight were executed.